# THE NAME GAME

## A LOOK BEHIND THE LABELS

BY
### DONNA M. JACKSON

ILLUSTRATED BY
### TED STEARN

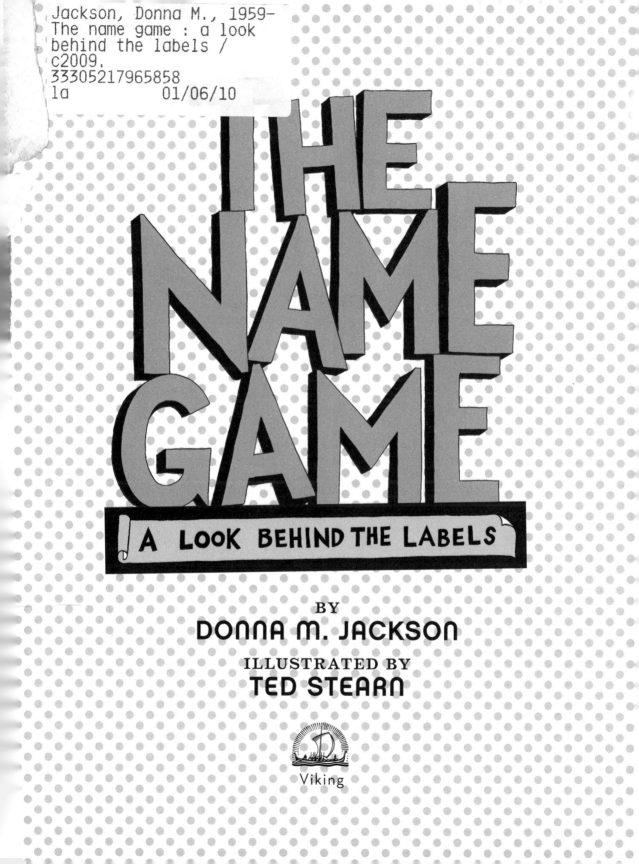

Viking

VIKING

Published by Penguin Group

Penguin Young Readers Group, 345 Hudson Street, New York, New York 10014, U.S.A.

Penguin Group (Canada), 90 Eglinton Avenue East, Suite 700, Toronto, Ontario, Canada M4P 2Y3
(a division of Pearson Penguin Canada Inc.)

Penguin Books Ltd, 80 Strand, London WC2R 0RL, England

Penguin Ireland, 25 St Stephen's Green, Dublin 2, Ireland (a division of Penguin Books Ltd)

Penguin Group (Australia), 250 Camberwell Road, Camberwell, Victoria 3124, Australia
(a division of Pearson Australia Group Pty Ltd)

Penguin Books India Pvt Ltd, 11 Community Centre, Panchsheel Park, New Delhi - 110 017, India

Penguin Group (NZ), 67 Apollo Drive, Rosedale, North Shore 0632, New Zealand (a division of Pearson New Zealand Ltd.)

Penguin Books (South Africa) (Pty) Ltd, 24 Sturdee Avenue, Rosebank, Johannesburg 2196, South Africa

Penguin Books Ltd, Registered Offices: 80 Strand, London WC2R 0RL, England

First published in 2009 by Viking, a division of Penguin Young Readers Group

1  3  5  7  9  10  8  6  4  2

Text copyright © Donna M. Jackson, 2009
Illustrations copyright © Ted Stearn, 2009
LIBRARY OF CONGRESS CATALOGING-IN-PUBLICATION DATA
Jackson, Donna M., date–
The name game : a look behind the labels / by Donna M. Jackson ; illustrations by Ted Stearn.
p. cm.
Includes index.
ISBN 978-0-670-01197-1 (hardcover)
1. Names—Juvenile literature. I. Title.
P323.J297 2009
929.9'7—dc22
2008037705

Manufactured in China
Set in Caslon
Book design by Nancy Brennan

WITH LOVE to the new kids on the block:
Victoria, Matthew, and Jacob,
Bobby Jr., Leah, Crystal, Sean, Kyle, Tiffany, Hailey, and Nicholas,
Eric, Adam, and Crystal,
and especially Christopher

In memory also of
Rose Elisabeth Reitman,
a beautiful girl with a lovely name

●　　●　　●

## Acknowledgments

A HEARTFELT THANK YOU to all who shared their knowledge about names for the book: Cleveland Kent Evans, Ph.D.; Jennifer Moss at BabyNames.com, who not only spoke with me, but also generously conducted an informal survey of her membership for the book; Lewis P. Lipsitt, Ph.D.; the folks at the American Name Society (www.wtsn.binghamton.edu/ANS), especially Don L. F. Nilsen and Alleen Pace Nilsen, co-presidents; Dean Vaughn of Dean Vaughn Learning Systems, Inc.; Burt Alper at Catchword Branding Company; Andy Chuang at Good Characters, Inc.; Carol Lombard; Fred Daniel of the Fred Society; Terry F. Godlove, Ph.D.; Alan Heavens, Ph.D.; Scott Speed; Kay Lagerquist, Ph.D.; Elayne Rapping; Miriam Ramos and Jacque Lynn Schultz at the ASPCA; Cathy Strange; Dr. Lynn M. Strange; Crystal Chasse; Jennifer and Zack Lane; and Sheri Stritof.

I'm especially grateful to Regina Hayes and Catherine Frank at Viking for their encouragement and enthusiastic support of this onomastic venture; to Ted Stearn for his clever illustrations; to Nancy Brennan for her vibrant design; and to Charlie Jackson, whose name I've proudly shared for more than a quarter of a century.

# Contents

The beginning of wisdom is to call things by their right names.

—*CHINESE PROVERB*

## 🔍 What's in a name?

POWER, IDENTITY, INFLUENCE. Hopes, dreams, history.

The Romans believed that *Nomen est omen*—in essence, a name is destiny. Some experts say names subtly sway our interests and career choices. They think it's one reason Scott Speed races cars and Alan Bloom tends to plants. It may also be why many Phils live in Philadelphia, Louis's live in St. Louis, and Georges live in St. George.

Others say names shape how we see ourselves and influence the expectations of those around us. A man named Bruno would have a tough time landing a job as a hair stylist, suggests one study. But his traditionally masculine name would serve him well if he wanted to work as a truck driver.

Likewise, a dog named Rambo is more apt to evoke fearful images than a dog named Muffin. Different names carry different connotations or implied meanings, according to psychologist James Bruning of Ohio University, and people use these meanings to make judgments.

In many religions, when you give something a name, "you give it existence," notes Howard Shepherd of "The Word Nerds," a podcast about language. In the Bible's book of Genesis for example, says Shepherd, "God says, 'Let there be light, and there is light.'" Another example of the power of names is the Jewish tradition, where "God's name is so holy that it can't be spoken," he says. "The four letters in the Hebrew alphabet that refer to God—the Tetragrammaton—are so sacred that you can't even speak them." Instead, people use a substitute such as *Ha-Shem*, which translates as "the name."

Communities past and present believe that knowing a person's name grants you power over him or her. Many African cultures give a child two names—one that's public and another that's kept secret to ward away evil spirits.

Ancient Hawaiians believed names were not only entities that people possessed but ones that possessed them as well. "Once spoken, the inoa [name] assumed a mystical existence and the power to help or harm the bearer," writes Eileen M. Root in her book, *Hawaiian Names . . . English Names*. "The more a name was spoken, the more powerful it became, and the more powerful its influence—good or evil."

"Names . . . distinguish us; they present us to others," writes author Deirdre McNamer. (Yes, that's her real name.) "Before you know much at all about a stranger, you know the stranger's name."

Our names are an integral part of our identity, says Cleveland Kent Evans, an associate psychology professor at Bellevue University and a past president of the American Name Society—an organization that promotes onomastics, the study of names and naming practices. Even those who claim not to like their name, he says, usually can't imagine changing it because it's so much a part of their identity.

# 🔍 Choosing Wisely

NO DOUBT, TODAY'S parents-to-be who live in the Western part of the world believe in the power of names. A 2007 survey conducted by BabyCenter, LLC, found that 58 percent of parents "believe a child's name contributes to his or her success in life," and choosing a name was one of their first major challenges as new moms and dads. Baby-name books and Web sites have also skyrocketed in popularity during the past decade. BabyNames.com, for example, welcomes a million and a half visitors each month, says the site's founder and chief executive officer, Jennifer Moss.

Moss believes parents have always put a lot of love and care into naming their children, but she says the Internet adds a community dimension. "Now you have the opportunity to see [name] statistics and get feedback from people other than your friends and family," she says. Then there's the Google factor. Prospective parents can now type their favorite names into search engines to see how popular they are and note who and what pops up.

When moms and dads find themselves really stuck—say, they don't agree on a name or they need help selecting a middle name—they can, and often do, call in the experts. After receiving "hundreds of e-mails every week" from people asking for

HER NAME IS "IGGIMPOOPOOWUMPY!"

IT WAS THE FIRST THING SHE EVER SAID!

help naming their babies, Moss began offering a name consulting service—one of many now available.

What should parents consider so that they—and their children—live happily ever after with a name?

Try not to get too creative with the spelling, says Moss, because your child will have to spell it for others the rest of his or her life. "Consider the sound and flow of the name. . . . One thing we recommend is to introduce yourself as your child. 'Hello, my name is . . .' then say the first and last name. How does that sound out loud? Is it hard to say? Is it easy to say? Does it sound like a tongue twister? Does it sound like something else, such as Crystal Chandelier?

"Then we say, pick a name that's important to you—maybe one that's from your history or your past, or just a name that you love. . . . Make sure you stay true to yourself."

Cleveland Kent Evans, author of *The Great Big Book of Baby Names*, also advises parents to ask themselves a few questions before deciding on a name.

- Is the name easy to remember?
- What nicknames are associated with it?
- Will the child's initials form an embarrassing word?
- Does the name itself have an inappropriate meaning, such as "Furious" or "Jealousy?" (names given to children in recent years).

Most of all, he says, parents should be especially conscious of why they're selecting a child's name. No matter what inspires it—ancestors, religious customs, or the media—"it helps the child's sense of identity and self-esteem for parents to have some story that's a bit more complicated than 'we just liked it,'" he says. It shows they put some thought behind the process.

Even then, there are no guarantees. After months of deliberating and narrowing down the choices, some parents experience "baby-name remorse" and change their child's name within a few months to a few years. "Emma seemed pretty," one mother told a reporter. "But it just felt strange coming out of my mouth"—even after mailing birth announcements. Today her daughter's name is Caroline.

"Perhaps one reason parents spend so much energy deciding on a name is that a child's physique, temperament, and talents are fundamentally out of their control," says Dr. Robert Needlman, a pediatrician for the Dr. Spock Company. "The name is one thing that they can actually determine."

It not only reflects a parent's values, but often conveys dreams and

expectations they have for their children. A name also can say "I love you" to a child, says Evans, and show how much you want to give him or her a good start in life. While names such as "Ura Scholar," "Good Kidd," and "Pleasant Lee" send obvious messages, the more popular monikers of Faith, Hope, Sage, and Earnest also do some talking.

Still, not everybody takes names quite so seriously—at least judging from the book of *Bad Baby Names* by Michael Sherrod and Matthew Rayback. Some parents enjoy pushing conventional boundaries by anointing their bundles of joy with names such as Leafy Green, Patty Cake, Marsha Mello, and Peter Rabbitt.

Sherrod mainly credits dads—past and present—with yielding to their funnybones. "I can't tell you how often I've heard guys who wanted their kid to be able to say truthfully, 'Danger is my middle name,'" he told *The New York Times.*

Experts say most people wear unusual names as well as any other. How individuals react to their names depends on a variety of factors, they explain, including how people feel about themselves. Some embrace unique names; others resist.

Still, some names test a child's emotional limits. One nine-year-old girl in New Zealand named Talula Does the Hula From Hawaii was so embarrassed by her name, she hid it from her friends and asked them to call her "K." A judge eventually ordered her name be changed, saying it set her up "with a social disability and handicap unnecessarily."

In another instance from the book *Freakonomics*, authors Steven D. Levitt and Stephen J. Dubner tell the story of two brothers—one named Winner, and the other named Loser. If names alone determined success, they asked, how could Winner fail and Loser triumph in life?

Yet that's just what happened. Today, Lou, as many co-workers call him, is a successful sergeant detective in the New York Police Department. And his sure-thing brother? He opted for a life of crime.

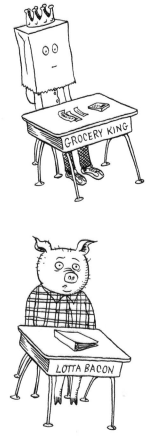

# Celebrity Baby Names

MAYBE STARS CRAVE more attention. Perhaps they're expressing their creativity and hoping to pass it along to their children. Whatever the reason, celebrities often push traditional naming limits to the innovative edge.

Take, for example, Moxie CrimeFighter. "You're likely to be the only one in any normal-size group with that name," magician and comedian Penn Jillette told *The New York Times* regarding the name of his daughter. "'Moxie' is a name that was created by an American for the first national soft drink and then went on to mean 'chutzpah,' and that's nice."

MORE OUT-OF-THE-ORDINARY CELEBRITY BABY NAMES INCLUDE:

APPLE BLYTHE ALISON MARTIN—
daughter of musician Chris Martin and actor Gwyneth Paltrow

AUDIO SCIENCE CLAYTON—
son of Dallas Clayton and actor Shannyn Sossamon

BANJO PATRICK TAYLOR—
son of artist Andrew Taylor and actor Rachel Griffiths

DAISY BOO OLIVER—
daughter of TV chef Jamie Oliver and model Juliette Norton

JERMAJESTY JACKSON—
son of musician Jermaine Jackson and Alejandra Oaziaza

KYD MILLER DUCHOVNY—
son of actors David Duchovny and Téa Leoni

PILOT INSPEKTOR RIESGRAF-LEE—
son of actors Jason Lee and Beth Riesgraf

SPECK WILDHORSE MELLENCAMP—
son of musician John Cougar Mellencamp and model Elaine Irwin

TU SIMONE AYER MORROW—
daughter of actors Rob Morrow and Debbon Ayer

ZUMA NESTA ROCK ROSSDALE—
son of musicians Gavin Rossdale and Gwen Stefani

# 🔍 Blackfoot Storytellers

EVERY NAME TELLS a story in the Blackfoot Indian culture. Not just any story—but a living, breathing, uniquely personal account that sends a message to others about who a person is and what he or she is expected to be. The names encourage people to live productive lives for their own benefit as well as their neighbors', says Carol Lombard, a master's degree candidate in sociolinguistics at the University of South Africa.

The Blackfoot Indians live mainly in Montana and in Alberta, Canada. The name Blackfoot is the English translation of the word "siksika"—*sik* meaning black, and *ika* meaning foot. Theories abound about the origins of the Blackfoot name. Some believe it refers to the dark moccasins the people wear, while others say it's a reference to the footprints left behind from those moccasins.

When a Blackfoot child is born, the family can take several months to select his or her name. Once a name is chosen—usually by the grandparents or great-grandparents—the family may hold a naming ceremony. During the celebration, the name is transferred as "a prayer [and a blessing] for that child to have a good life, to be successful, and very importantly, to be able to contribute to the community," says Lombard. Names also reflect a spiritual aspect of traditional Blackfoot culture, she says, "in that a name is actually seen as a protecting force over the child as he or she grows up."

Blackfoot women generally carry their birth names all their lives. But Blackfoot men—while keeping one "legal" name for convenience in Western society—traditionally undergo several name changes within the tribe, explains Lombard. Each name change reflects a new phase of life. A young boy, for instance, may carry his name into adolescence or his early twenties, and then, as his parents or grandparents see his accomplishments, they may decide it's time for him to take on a new name so that he can develop further. As time goes on and people continue to watch where the man takes his life, they may encourage him to change his name again, "so he can grow even more," says Lombard. "And so it may continue until quite late in life."

New names arise not only from accomplishments but also from ancestors. It's very important to carry family names, says Lombard, so the spirit and memories of one's ancestors live on. Often names are given out with stories about the ancestors, stories about who they were and how they lived their lives. So if a boy is given his grandfather's name, along with his story, it gives him a strong sense of identity. "But stories are always told for a purpose." If your grandfather achieved certain things, and you were told about them, then this conveys what's expected of you as you carry the name forward. "There's the past, and then there's what you're doing with that name in the present, and what you are going to do with that name in the future," says Lombard. "When the name is transferred, all the stories that go along with it are transferred too. And it's in those stories that you get the history, meaning, and implications of that name."

**"NYM" WORDS:** The root -onym or -nym originates from the Greek word *onoma*, which means name. When a prefix is added to -nym, the resulting word often refers to a specific type of name, such as patronym—a name derived from a person's father or paternal ancestor. Or a -nym word can describe the relationship between words or names. Antonyms, for example, are words with opposite meanings.

# Firsts, Lasts, and Middles

ONCE UPON A time, the world was filled with Adams and Eves and Johns and Pauls and Marys. People identified themselves by their first, or given names. Nothing more was required.

As the population grew, so did the number of men and women with the same names, making it difficult to distinguish them from one another. To simplify life, people began using surnames—from the French word *surnom*—where *sur* means "in addition to" the name. No one knows exactly when surnames were first used, but they began gaining popularity in Europe around the twelfth century. In European and European-influenced countries, such as the United States and Australia, surnames are family names that follow given names. In Eastern countries, such as China and Japan, surnames are family names placed *before* the given name.

Nearly all surnames in Western cultures fall into one of four categories, explains Don Nilsen, professor of English Linguistics at Arizona State University and co-president of the American Name Society:

○ Patronymics—formed from the father's first or given name, such as Ericson, meaning the son of Eric.

- Occupational names—arising from a person's trade, such as Smith for a blacksmith or Thatcher for a person who thatches roofs.
- Topographical names—formed from geographical features or the area where a person lives, such as Underhill, Woods, or Fields.
- Names derived from personal characteristics—originating from individual traits, such as Short, Brown, or Small.

Once surnames took hold, middle names began popping up in England around the sixteenth century. "Middle names honored a maternal line, gave an alternative to a common or disliked 'first name,' or could perk up a plain name," such as "William French Smith," writes author Leonard R. N. Ashley in *What's in a Name?*

They can also be a "side effect" from naming children after famous people, notes onomastician (names expert) Cleveland Kent Evans. "At the beginning of the Revolutionary War, people in the United States wanted to name their sons George" in honor of George Washington, he says. The problem was, King George III of England was still around. To keep things clear, parents added Washington in as a middle name. "Gradually, in the course of about a hundred years, middle names became the custom," he says. "By the Civil War, it was unusual in the United States if you didn't have a middle name," and it remains so today.

# Icelandic Traditions

STOP, IN THE name of the law! That's what some countries tell parents when they select baby names that don't make the grade.

In Iceland, for instance, the Icelandic Naming Committee reviews and approves given names to ensure they fit into cultural traditions and meet certain language and grammatical requirements. One name the government would probably reject is Zeke, because it contains the letter *Z*, which is not in the Icelandic alphabet.

Icelanders also follow an unusual system for first and last names. Since the days of the Vikings, fathers—and sometimes mothers—have directly passed down their first names to their children, not their last. For example, if Jón Helgason had a son, the boy's last name would be Jónsson, meaning the son of Jón. If Jón Helgason had a daughter, the girl's last name would be Jónsdóttir, meaning the daughter of Jón. Since Icelandic women do not take their husband's names when they marry, one family with the same mother and father could have four different last names.

JÓN HELGASON

JONA ERICSDÓTTIR

JÓN JÓNSSON    JONA JÓNSDÓTTIR

# Chinese Surnames

WHEN A CHINESE name is written in Chinese, the surname is always placed before the given name. "This practice is also adopted by the Korean and Japanese," explains naming expert Andy Chuang. "Most have names entirely based on Chinese characters. The Korean's adaptation of Chinese characters is called hanja, and the Japanese version is kanji."

When a Chinese name is transliterated—changed into the corresponding characters of another alphabet—there's no easy way to tell whether the surname is being placed first or last, says Chuang. For example, basketball player Yao Ming's family name is Yao, and his given name is Ming. On the other hand, cellist Yo-Yo Ma's family name is Ma, and his given name is Yo-Yo.

"A general rule is that political figures and famous Chinese people who don't speak much English spell their names the way they sound in Chinese, and that those who live in the West or who are able to communicate directly with the press often choose to spell and arrange their names the Western way," says Chuang.

Traditionally, Chinese fathers pass their family names to their children. But Chinese women—who keep their surnames when they marry—may also pass on their family names. In addition, Chinese laws may soon allow parents to combine their surnames and create new, blended names for their children. In 2007, officials announced

they may authorize the ground-breaking practice, because there's a huge shortage of surnames in the country.

About 85 percent of China's 1.3 billion citizens share 100 surnames, according to a nationwide Chinese survey. This includes 93 million with the surname Wang, 92 million with the surname Li, and 88 million with the surname Zhang. Combining the family names of Chinese parents could add as many as 1.28 million new naming possibilities, reports *China Daily*, an English-language newspaper published in China. "A father named Zhou and [a] mother named Zhu," for instance, "could choose to call their child either Zhou, Zhu, Zhouzhu or Zhuzhou."

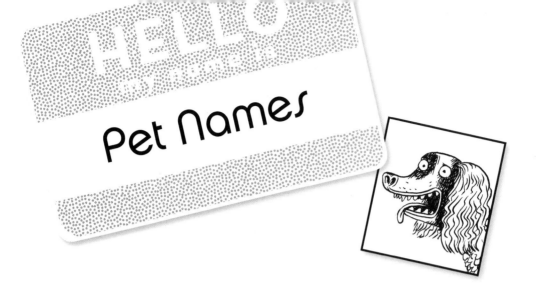

# Pet Names

"We picked up a tiny, white, odd-eyed kitten some years back. The cat was deaf, so we just naturally named [it] Say What?"

—Terry von Gease, in *The Complete Book of Pet Names*

IN THE PET world, names pack a big bite. Not only do they serve as signs of love and respect, they're powerful attention-getters. That's one reason Jacque Lynn Schultz of the American Society for the Prevention of Cruelty to Animals (ASPCA) recommends keeping pet names short and sweet.

Simplify your pet's life and give him or her a one- or two-syllable name that's easy to recognize, such as Max or Sheba, she says. Short names can be especially helpful with obedience-training a dog. "Just be sure to say the dog's name at the beginning of the command. This way your pet will know you're talking to him and not someone else in the room."

It's also important to select a name you'll feel comfortable calling out in front of other people, says Schultz, who is the senior director of the ASPCA's National Outreach program. "Poo-poo," for example, might be a little embarrassing. "Realize that your pet's name reflects on the animal *and* back at you."

Other pet-naming tips from Schultz include:

- Avoid names that sound similar to voice commands, such as *no, sit, heel*, and *come*. Joey would probably work better than Joe, she says.

- Think twice about scary names, such as Jaws or Killer, for large dogs like Rottweilers and German shepherds. "You won't be helping the dog's reputation," she says, and people may run in the opposite direction.

- Pick names that will grow with your pets, not ones that only work well while the animals are young.

- Consider names based on the pet's breed or physical characteristics, such as Kelly for an Irish Setter or Patches for a multi-colored cat, Spike for a cockatiel, Mocha for a rabbit, Sequoia for a horse, and Pretzel for a snake.

- Consider names based on a pet's personality, such as Shadow for a dog who likes to follow you everywhere. Schultz has a two-year-old cat she named Bop-the-Cat (nicknamed Bop or Boppy), in part, because he likes to "Be Bop"

out the door every chance he gets. Her dog, Harpo, is named after the silent Marx brother "because he's pretty clowny and doesn't bark much."

- Be creative. Look to art (Picasso), music (Banjo), literature (Frodo), mythology (Zeus), movies (Keiko), nature (Bamboo), science (Einstein), other languages (Kito, a Swahili name for a male, meaning precious), food (Cashew), and even brand-names of appliances as one woman did (Maytag), in your search to find the perfect name for your pet!

OH, THE PLACES you can go! You can get lost in a Story (Virginia), check out a Rembrandt (Iowa), or find sweet Harmony (California). You can visit Brothers and Sisters (Oregon), Lewis and Clark (Missouri), and Romulus and Remus (Michigan). Looking for a place that's out of this world? Try flying to the Moon (Kentucky), the North Star (Minnesota), or Neptune (New Jersey).

If you get hungry along the way, your stomach may lead you to Two Egg (Florida)—named in the 1800s by a traveling salesman who noticed townspeople typically traded a couple of eggs for candy and other items at the general store.

Need something to go with those eggs?

You might try some Oatmeal (Texas), Toast (North Carolina), Cereal (Illinois), Bacon (Georgia), or possibly a Pancake (Pennsylvania). Top it off with a large selection of fruit: Apple (Ohio), Grape (Michigan), Mango (Florida), Melon (Texas), Blueberry (Wisconsin), Blackberry (Minnesota), Nectarine (Pennsylvania), and plenty of Cherries, Oranges, and Strawberries (from Connecticut to California).

Perhaps you'd rather eat lunch, with Chili (Indiana) and a piece of

Pie (West Virginia) in Greasy Corner (Arkansas). Or feast on a Hero (Pennsylvania) Sandwich (Massachusetts) piled high with layers of Chicken (Alaska) and Turkey (Texas), topped with Swiss (Missouri) cheese, Tomato (Arkansas), and some Olives—hold the Mayo (Louisiana) of course.

It's all sure to be Yum Yum (Tennessee)!

TOPONYM: a place name—such as Florida—or a name that's derived from a place. The word hamburger stems from the city of Hamburg, Germany.

# That's a Mouthful

LAKE CHARGOGGAGOGGMANCHAUGGAGOGGCHAUBUNAGUNGAMAUGG. That's right, says reporter Pam Belluck of *The New York Times*. "It is spelled just the way it sounds." The Massachusetts lake holds the distinction of having the longest place name in the United States. Chargoggagoggmanchauggagoggchaubunagungamaugg officially means "English knifemen and Nipmuck Indians at the boundary or neutral fishing place," according to one local historian. But people around the world know it by its more humorous—and inaccurate—translation: "You fish on your side, I fish on my side, and nobody fishes in the middle."

## Blowing in the Wind

"One of the first human records of hurricanes appears in Mayan hieroglyphics. . . . In fact, it is the Mayan word 'Hurakan' that became our word 'hurricane.' Hurakan was the name of one of their gods, who, they believed, blew his breath across the water and brought forth dry land. Later, Carib Indians gave the name 'Hurican' to one of their gods of evil."—The History of Hurricanes, FEMA for Kids

KATRINA. ANDREW. GLORIA. IKE.

Historic hurricanes few will forget. By naming these destructive storms, the World Meteorological Organization (WMO) helps people keep track of them from start to finish, and the name serves as a valuable identifier for years beyond.

Hurricanes are severe tropical weather systems—generically called tropical cyclones—that generate heavy rains and spiraling winds of 74 miles per hour or more. The violent storms form over warm seas in seven regions of the world, called basins, and are identified as hurricanes, typhoons, or cyclones depending on where they originate.

No matter where in the world a storm strikes, however, it's assigned a special name—technically called an anemonym (which literally means name of a wind). This makes it easier for meteorologists, researchers, insurance specialists, and the general public to reference and follow its path.

Names for hurricanes, typhoons, and cyclones are generally short, simple, and easy to pronounce, says Gary Padgett, author of the worldwide Monthly Global Tropical Cyclone Summaries. The names also are commonly known within each of the global formation basins, with some weather services—including the National Weather Center and the Hong Kong Observatory—offering glossaries and pronunciation guides on the Internet.

Early on, people living in the Caribbean Islands named hurricanes after the various saints' days in the Catholic Church. Hurricane Santa Ana, for example, struck Puerto Rico on July 26, 1825, which is the designated feast day of Saint Ann.

Later, people used numbers—longitude and latitude—but those proved to be "cumbersome and confusing," says Padgett. "This was especially true when several storms brewed in the same basin."

During World War II, when the U.S. Navy began flying scouting missions into Western Pacific typhoons, they began naming the storms alphabetically after women—most often wives and loved ones. The practice is thought to have originated in the late 1800s with an Australian meteorological director named Clement Wragge, who also is credited with naming winter storms after politicians he didn't like.

In 1953, the U.S. National Weather Service also adopted a female-naming strategy. That decade, hurricanes Hazel, Connie, and Diane wreaked havoc along the Atlantic coast. It wasn't until 1979 that male names such as David, Henri, and Frederic were added to the list.

Today, hurricanes and tropical storm names alternate alphabetically between men and women's names, with one name for every letter except *Q, U, X, Y,* and *Z.* The World Meteorological Organization, which coordinates regional committees to name storms in all basins, uses six lists of hurricane names that it rotates every year. Names selected may be English, French, Spanish, and sometimes Dutch, to reflect the major languages spoken in countries that border the Atlantic Ocean. When a hurricane is particularly deadly or destructive, its name is retired and a new one selected. The name Katrina, for example, will never be used again and has been replaced with Katia.

What happens when forecasters run out of names on the list during one season? Well then, it's time to go to the Greek alphabet and say hello to hurricanes Alpha, Beta, Gamma, Delta, Epsilon, and Zeta. This scenario occurred in 2005, when a record-breaking twenty-seven named storms formed in the Atlantic.

CRYPTONYM: a secret or code name, often used in the military and by computer companies. Nintendo's video game console, Wii, was secretly named "Revolution" while it was being developed.

# The Art of Naming Companies

> "The most important branding decision you will ever make is what to name your product or service. . . . All other factors being equal, the brand with the better name will come out on top."
>
> —Al Ries and Laura Ries, *The 22 Immutable Laws of Branding*

NAMES ARE FIRST impressions, an opportunity to knock the customer's socks off—or persuade them to try on a new pair, if that's what you're selling. A name's the first chance you have to communicate with potential customers, says Burt Alper, one of the founding members of Catchword, a naming company that specializes in developing brand names.

Just as nametags help introduce people at parties, brand names are a way for businesses to "shake hands with a customer," he says. Good names will reflect positively on the brand. They'll reflect the associations and messages that a business wants customers to have about their company or products, he says. Bad names will not.

Take Nike, says Alper. "It's a good name because it's distinctive, trustworthy, and short—four letters and two syllables." Nike's also "the goddess

of victory. Not everyone knows that." For those who do, the name's particularly relevant, he says.

On the other hand, there's Yahoo! While the name's "short, very fun, and has the right energy," he says, "it has a derogatory meaning in most parts of the country. A yahoo is someone you don't take seriously . . . so the name doesn't really say 'we're the place you should go to with questions.'"

What makes a great business name? It depends, in part, on the company or product, says Alper, who holds degrees in business and psycholinguistics—the study of how people understand, interpret, and respond to language. Besides being short and distinctive, the best names are easy to pronounce and simple to remember. They magnify the message you want to communicate about the benefits of your product, he says. "If your name sounds easy, friendly, and approachable, that's a good reinforcement for the brand."

THERONYM: a name—usually of a product—that's derived from the name of an animal, such as the Ford Mustang.

Global appeal is also important—although few names will perform well across every language, says Alper. It depends on the market. "If you're going from the United States to Australia, some innuendoes are different, but the language is the same. If you're going from the United States to China, you have different languages to address . . . and it's a lot harder to get any sort of relevance across those multiple language groups."

That's where the skills of people such as Andy Chuang, president of Good Characters, Inc., come in handy. Chuang tests potential business names to ensure they're appropriate in the three most widely spoken Chinese languages: Mandarin, the official Chinese language; Min Nan, also referred to as Taiwanese or Hokkien; and Cantonese.

"For example, Hewlett-Packard's Chinese branding [name] is Hui-Pu," says Chuang. "Hui is 'kindness' and Pu, 'universal.' So Hui-Pu can mean 'benefit to all.' It sounds somewhat like Hewlett-Packard and has a good meaning that fits the company's philosophy and position."

# ☉ Building Brands

NAMING IS MORE of an art than a science, explains Alper, who's been in the business ten years. When developing names, the Catchword team follows a three-step process. First, there's the discovery stage, "where we learn about what we're naming and identify the messages we want to communicate," he says.

Next is the creative exploration stage. During this phase, team members research and generate thousands of naming possibilities based on the information they've been given. When all lists are pulled together, the group moves into the third stage of the process—screening and filtering names. "This is where we weed out the names that aren't going to work because they have some negative or unfortunate meaning, or they're difficult to pronounce, or we just plain don't like them," Alper says.

The team also checks various databases to see what other companies might be using the name and to ensure the availability of trademarks—names that can be legally registered—and domain names, which are unique names that identify Web sites, such as cnn.com. "We get it down to a short list of finalists, and take it from there until we have a winner," he says.

When creating a name for their company, none of the founders chose Catchword as their first favorite. "But it was in the top three for each of us," says Alper. "It was the highest common denominator." Forty-eight hours after making their selection, the team forgot all about the other finalists. "You start to fall in love with the name soon after you select it," he says. "It happens all the time."

- Diet Deluxe to Healthy Choice
- Hertz Drive-Ur-Self System to Hertz Rent-a-Car
- Computing Tabulating-Recording Corporation to IBM (International Business Machines)
- Marufuku Company to Nintendo Playing Card Company to Nintendo
- Blue Ribbon Sports to Nike
- Quantum Computer Services to America Online to AOL
- Service Game Company to Sega

"SMART, NICE, QUIET, accomplished."

An impressive achiever with whom nobody stays in touch. Were all Grace Lees brilliant but forgettable? That's the question filmmaker Grace Lee posed in her 2005 award-winning documentary, "The Grace Lee Project."

Growing up in Missouri, Grace Lee stood out in the crowd as "the only Asian girl for miles." But when the Midwesterner moved to California, she discovered a whole new world of Grace Lees—from pianists to prodigies. The experience triggered an identity crisis that left her wondering how she fit in.

Determined to differentiate herself and find a few Grace Lees who broke the "statistical average" of an American-born, single Korean woman, about five feet three inches tall, and twenty-five years of age, with at least one college degree, she began searching for namesakes. Among the more than two thousand Grace Lees living in the United States and countless others across the globe, she found a TV news reporter, a cruise-ship singer, a pastor's wife, and a feisty ninety-two-year-old social activist from Detroit named Grace Lee Boggs.

GRACE LEE
#254

GRACE LEE
#363

GRACE LEE
#1864

GRACE LEE
#28

GRACE LEE
#981

GRACE LEE
#122

GRACE LEE
#1650

GRACE LEE
#6

GRACE LEE
#1659

GRACE LEE
#1310

GRACE LEE
#812

GRACE LEE
#54

# 🔍 Virtual Links

GRACE LEE'S NOT the only person curious about her alter egos. Many people Google themselves to see if—and where—their name ranks on the hit list, as well as to check out the "competition." These same-name cyber clones are called Googlegängers—a term created by combining Google and the German word *Doppelgänger,* which refers to a person's double or look-alike. Oddly enough, most people feel a mysterious kinship with their virtual twins.

One reason for the connection may be a phenomenon called the "name-letter effect," where we unconsciously prefer people, places, and things that contain the letters in our own names, notes psychologist Brett Pelham. This probably explains groups such as the FRED Society, the World Wide Wendys, and the Jerry Hill Club.

Jim Killeen of California felt such a strong bond with his Googlegängers that he tracked down six of them—from Ireland to Australia—and made a movie about it called *Google Me.* After meeting the other Jim Killeens and learning about their diverse lives, he decided names are simply labels. Although we strongly identify with our names and use them to interact with the world, he says, "I don't think you can use [them] to tell that much about a person."

Filmmaker Grace Lee also made some surprising discoveries during her self-search. Today, she no longer fears being mistaken for another Grace Lee. In fact, she says, "I can't wait to meet the rest of us!"

Mononym: a one-word name, such as Beyoncé.

# Screen Personas

AT SEVENTEEN, JENNIFER Lane wanted a screen name with a little sass, so she picked "sweetkisses," paired with a number. Her fifteen-year-old brother, Zack, wanted something cool, so he went with "cornmuffin." Creating a screen name for Instant Messaging (IM) can be a playful process "because you can make them as funny or silly as you want," says Zack, and "no one will make fun of you for it."

Finding the perfect handle takes a little time and effort, however. Most teens aim for names that are catchy, creative, and reflect a piece of their personality. "Artzyfartzy," "pawprints," and "mountainbird," for example, echo the interests and imaginations of their users.

When Crystal Chasse chose her first screen name at thirteen, she collaborated with friends to come up with "CrazyAngel"—a name that reflected her spirited persona. A few years later, she tweaked the name to "CrazyCryst," adding the alliteration and keeping the emphasis on her more fun-loving qualities.

Many teens juggle several screen names and email addresses—some more public than others. This helps them organize the various parts of their online lives, according to a 2006 survey conducted by the Pew Internet & American Life Project. It also allows them to try on different online identities and do things such as secretly ask for homework help.

Still, time has a way of weeding out unfortunate choices.

No matter what you choose while you're in school, says Jennifer Lane, who recently graduated from college, "you'll always regret it four years later."

# Name Exchange

SOME NAMES FIT perfectly. Others don't wear as well.

While many people learn to live with their mismatched monikers, a few take matters into their own hands and legally select new ones.

Changing your name in the United States generally involves a simple court procedure. Men, women, and children do it every day for a variety of reasons. Along with the desire for a more suitable signature, people often change their names when they marry, divorce, or adopt children. Life events such as these typically prompt tweaks that include the addition, subtraction, substitution, or hyphenation of a last name.

Some people change their names for practical reasons. One man whose real name was Stephen O found himself repeatedly being turned down for credit cards because computers didn't recognize his single-letter surname. He eventually added an *h* to his last name so he could move on with his life and do a little shopping.

Laws differ from state to state, but in general, people can modify their first, middle, or last names as long as they follow a few rules.

NAME-CHANGERS CANNOT:

- Change names with the intent to commit an illegal act, such as avoiding debts or hiding from the police.
- Use obscene or curse words.
- Use numbers or symbols (except for Roman numerals at the end of the name).
- Interfere with the rights of other people, such as celebrities, by trying to take on their names and use them to mislead.

# ⌕ Married Names

WHEN WEDDING BELLS ring, couples have all sorts of decisions to make, including how they'll label themselves in their partnership. Many women today choose to keep their family names in one form or another to preserve their identity and heritage, says Sheri Stritof, co-author of *The Everything Great Marriage Book* and marriage expert on About.com. "This is my name," some women tell Stritof. "It's who I am." While men generally are open to alternatives, she says, every now and then a conflict arises. One bride-to-be told Stritof her fiancé is

Dennis Dee
&
Doris Doo

Dennis Dee
&
Doris Dee

Dennis Dee
&
Doris Dee-Doo

Dennis Dee
&
Doris Dee Doo

Dennis Dee
&
Doris Doo/Dee

Dennis Doodee
&
Doris Doodee

upset because she won't take his last name. He's worried his conservative family won't accept the decision. Hopefully, the pair worked it out and decided on one of the many naming options available to all those who walk down the aisle. These include:

- The bride can take the groom's last name and drop her last name.
- The groom can take the bride's last name and drop his, which is happening more often these days.
- The bride can attach the groom's last name to hers with a hyphen.
- The bride and groom can each attach the other's name to theirs with a hyphen.
- The bride can convert her last name into a new middle name.
- The bride can keep her birth name professionally, but legally change it to her husband's last name.
- The bride and groom can both keep their own names.
- The bride and the groom can both change their names—blending the two together or creating something totally new and different.

## Claims to Fame

AS THEY RISE to the top, celebrities often change their names—or assume stage names—to match their professional personas. Hollywood starlets once were told to "use your middle name as your first name (and) the street where you grew up as your last," notes Jennifer Moss on BabyNames.com. Movie studio executives also tagged newcomers with names that were either more glamorous, such as Cyd Charisse for Tula Ellice Finklea, or more mainstream, such as Cary Grant for Archibald Alexander Leach.

Today, celebrities enjoy a bit more control over transforming their identities.

Alicia Augello-Cook's hunt for a more musically meaningful last name ended on a high note. After flipping through a dictionary and considering "Wild" for a short time, she decided on "Keys"—Alicia Keys. "It's like the piano keys," the Grammy winner told *Newsweek* magazine. "And it can open so many doors."

● ● ● NAME NIBBLES ● ● ●

## More Name Swappers

MILEY RAY CYRUS, singer = Destiny Hope Cyrus

DEMI MOORE, actor = Demetria Guynes

JAMIE FOXX, actor = Eric Bishop

FAITH HILL, singer = Audrey Faith Perry

MICHAEL CAINE, actor = Maurice Joseph Micklewhite

MUHAMMAD ALI, heavyweight boxing champ = Cassius Marcellus Clay, Jr.

QUEEN LATIFA, actor, singer = Dana Elaine Owens

TINA TURNER, singer = Anna Mae Bullock

WHOOPI GOLDBERG, actor, TV host = Caryn Elaine Johnson

Autonym: a person's real name, as opposed to a pseudonym.

# Destiny Calling

DAVID M. BIRD STUDIES raptors.

Alan Heavens works as an astronomer.

Les Plack—a dentist—fixes teeth.

Coincidence? Dr. Lewis Lipsitt of Brown University thinks maybe not. The psychology professor has been studying people whose names aptly describe their careers or hobbies for nearly fifty years. In this time, he's come to believe that simply hearing themselves called by such names—known as aptronyms—over and over again can subconsciously influence people's interests.

Dr. Lipsitt first developed his theory after pointing out in a class that people's names and occupations were *not* connected. He used aptronyms as an example of meaningless coincidence. Soon after, he began having second thoughts.

"At the time, Dr. Fish, Mr. Seeman and Mr. Saila were three of the founding members of the Rhode Island Oceanographic Institute; Dr. Hawkes was head of the Audubon Society; Mr. Rolls was head of the

Rhode Island Automobile Association; Mrs. Record kept the alumni records at Brown University; and Mr. Fidler taught in the music department. And so on. I kept going with a few more examples when a student blurted out: 'And you—you, Dr. Lipsitt, study the sucking behavior of babies!' Why then, I was convinced that there must be a causal connection. These could not all be coincidences, in the sense of chance pairings."

Through the years, Dr. Lipsitt has collected thousands of aptronym examples—many of which friends and former students have sent to him. Among his favorites are Dr. Doctor, Attorney Lawyer, Professor Wisdom, and Dr. Ogle, a vision specialist.

David M. Bird, a Canadian ornithologist, believes his name is an asset to his profession, but insists it wasn't a factor early on.

Terry Godlove, professor of philosophy and religion at Hofstra University, also remains unconvinced his name influenced his career choice—although he admits it may have prompted some to notice his resume more along the way. "Godlove is a literal translation of a very common German name, Gottlieb," he explains. Still, he can't help but find some life coincidences a bit curious and amusing. These include the fact that he studied philosophy at Oberlin College with the likes of "Norman Care, David Love, and Daniel Grimm" and that he currently lives on Puritan Avenue.

APTRONYM: a name aptly suited to its owner's occupation or interests, such as baseball player Prince Fielder.

# What's Up, Doc?

WHILE SOME PEOPLE pick professions that complement their names, others choose careers that seemingly defy them. Psychologist Lewis Lipsitt believes this could be a defense mechanism called reaction formation—where people subconsciously rebel against the messages their names imply. Whatever the reason, it can make for some memorable office visits!

- DR. STEPHANIE PAYNE, Dentist at Gentle Dental
- DR. SCOTT A. HACKER, Surgeon
- DR. ROBERT BONEBRAKE, Chiropractor
- DR. CATHERINE RUDE, Pediatrician
- DR. PATRICK RASH, Dermatologist
- DR. PAUL NURSE, Rockefeller University President and cancer researcher
- DR. MARK MEANEY, Advocate for patients rights
- DR. ROBERTA L. NUTT, Director of the doctoral counseling psychology program at Texas Woman's University

# Nicknames: Getting Personal

"Nicknames stick to people, and the most ridiculous are the most adhesive."
—Thomas C. Haliburton, Canadian author, 1796–1865

NICKNAMES CAN ENHANCE a reputation, as in "Honest Abe" Lincoln.

Or they can diminish a person's credibility, as in "Tricky Dick" Nixon.

They can be cool, as in "The Boss," or cruel as in "Baldy."

Some nicknames—referred to as pet names—bond close friends and family, serving as signs of intimacy and trust. Others poke at relationships with sarcasm ("Speedy" for someone who's slow) and illuminate flaws.

"We tend to think of nicknames as being slightly frivolous, even though they carry more freight than birth names," write Justin Kaplan and Anne Bernays in *The Language of Names: What We Call Ourselves and Why It Matters.* "They describe, record, imply, deride, or deplore something specific about the person to whom they are attached. Birth names, on the other hand, mainly say something about the people who attach them."

Originating from the Middle English phrase "an eke name," which means an additional or "also" name, nicknames have been around longer than surnames. Not surprisingly, many family names started as nicknames. Men—especially in music, the military, and sports—tend to give and receive nicknames more often than women, notes psychologist Cleveland Kent Evans. The tags—humorous or familiar—can be a non-threatening way for friends to show affection.

Nicknames take a variety of shapes. Some are simply short forms of given names, such as "Gabi" for Gabriela or "Nate" for Nathaniel. Others highlight physical traits, like Al "Scarface" Capone. They may reference a person's occupation or title, such as "Chief," or liken someone to an animal ("Moose") or literary figure ("Sherlock").

With the advent of instant messaging and cell phone technology, some teens have started calling their parents by casual,

BUTTERBALL

BOY BLUE

quirky nicknames such as Big Anne, G-Dad, and Mama Jo—all to mixed reviews.

In the Philippines, nearly everyone—young and old—has a colorful nickname. "In fact, it's perfectly acceptable (and not the least bit embarrassing) for Filipinos to take whimsical nicknames like Butterball, Boy Blue, or Pee-wee to the grave," according to *Psychology Today*. The names not only help differentiate Filipinos from each other, they foster a strong sense of community. One woman tells how her cousin's "perfect circle" face at birth earned her the nickname Bilog, which means round. "Even though it doesn't fit her anymore," says the woman, "she'll always be Bilog."

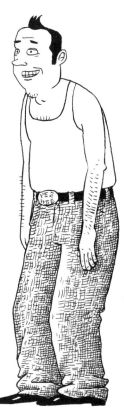

PEE-WEE

EPONYM: the name of a person—real or imagined—for which something is named. Tootsie Rolls were named after Clara "Tootsie" Hirshfield by her candy-making dad.

# Sports Tags

"You have to have a nickname to be remembered."

—James "Dusty" Rhodes, 1950s New York Giants

SPORTSCASTERS AND FANS eat them up. They're colorful and creative, and capture the essence of our athletic heroes. Some sports nicknames are so memorable they overshadow a person's actual name, notoriety, or achievements. Ultimately, however, sports tags help ensure a person's place in history—and often in our hearts.

- SHOELESS JOE JACKSON (Joe Jackson/baseball)
- PURPLE PEOPLE EATERS (Minnesota Vikings' 1960s and 70s defensive line/football)
- HAMMERIN' HANK (Hank Aaron/baseball)
- THE REFRIGERATOR (William Perry/football)
- THE GREAT ONE (Wayne Gretzky/hockey)
- THE BLACK WIDOW (Jeanette Lee/billiards)
- AIR JORDAN (Michael Jordan/basketball)
- OIL CAN BOYD (Dennis Boyd/baseball)
- MANOS DE PIEDRA or HANDS OF STONE (Roberto Duran/boxing)
- THE SPLENDID SPLINTER (Ted Williams/baseball)
- THE GOLDEN BEAR (Jack Nicklaus/golf)
- THE INTIMIDATOR (Dale Earnhardt/auto racing)

# Picture This ... Tips for Remembering Names

WANT TO IMPRESS someone? Know their name.

"People who remember names become more appreciated and popular," says Dean Vaughn, author of *How to Remember Anything.* Even people who *try* to recall names are viewed more favorably than those who give up and don't try at all.

Vaughn has spent most of his life developing memory and learning systems to help people in school and business. During a dinner banquet, he memorized the names of 223 people he met as they entered the dining room. After speaking to the group, he asked everyone to stand and then sit down as he called out their names. "No one was left standing," he says.

Fortunately, most of us only need to remember one or two names at a time—which is better than most people can do, he says. Below are a few of Vaughn's memory tips (called mnemonics) for recalling names like a pro.

- Think in word pictures: Change the person's name into a sound-alike word picture. For example, you might visualize a bunch of nickels for the name Nicholas. Images are much easier to recall than words, Vaughn says.

○ Get silly: The more ridiculous your sound-alike word picture, the more memorable the name will be. Let your imagination take flight and picture the person doing something crazy, such as skateboarding with the nickels.

○ Start a collection: Collect names and word pictures in a file, so you'll be ready next time you meet someone new. A set of cards with only one hundred names in each category—boys, girls, and even last names—will work for tens of thousands of people, says Vaughn. "It makes it really easy to remember names if you already have a word picture for the names of the people you meet." The same word picture, for example, works for all people named Nicholas.

Below are several names and word pictures to get your collection off to a good start.

| BOYS' NAMES | WORD PICTURE |
|---|---|
| 1. Aidan | aid (Band-Aid) |
| 2. Christopher | Christmas tree |
| 3. Jacob | "j" cup (a cup shaped like a "j") |
| 4. Luke | looking glass |
| 5. Nathan | gnat |

| GIRLS' NAMES | WORD PICTURE |
|---|---|
| 1. Ava | avenue |
| 2. Emily | a million leaves |
| 3. Hailey | hail |
| 4. Madison | medicine |
| 5. Olivia | olive |

NATE — BOY
(loves to play tennis)

NICHOLAS — BOY
5¢ 5¢
(loves to skateboard)

EMILY — GIRL
(loves being outside)

HAILEY — GIRL
(loves ice cream)

# 🔍 Did You Know?

- Celebrate Your Name Week is the first full week in March. It includes a Namesake Day, a Unique Names Day, and a Learn What Your Name Means Day.

- Many countries in Europe and Latin America celebrate "name days" much like birthdays—complete with cards, parties, and gifts. The practice originates from the Christian tradition of dedicating each day of the year to a saint or martyr. Name days honor first names that correspond to the feast days of saints. For example, the name day for Justin is June first, which is St. Justin's day.

- Names can make some people sick. Sufferers of a rare condition known as onomatophobia not only fear speaking particular names or words, they panic at the thought of seeing or hearing them.

- In Scotland, there was a doctor named Donald Duck. Born ten years before Walt Disney's cartoon character, Dr. Duck enjoyed his name and never considered changing it. Even so, he said, he wouldn't name any of his children Huey, Dewey, or Louie!

- All American states have one or more nicknames—some more official than others. Massachusetts, which is known as "The Bay State," has also been called "The Bean-Eating State." Utah, officially the "Beehive State,"  was nicknamed "The Good Highway State"; and Texas, "The Lone Star State," was once known as "America's Fun-tier."

Caconomenology is the study of ugly names. Several Web sites are devoted to collecting and highlighting "bad baby names."

Anagrams are words or phrases formed by reordering the letters in other words, including names. *Clint Eastwood* shuffles to *Old West action*, *Ralph Waldo Emerson* becomes *Person whom all read*, and *The Mona Lisa* transforms to *No hat, a smile*. In the Middle Ages, King Louis XIII of France took anagrams more seriously than most, writes author Paul Dickson. He hired a Royal Anagrammatist named Thomas Billon to "scramble and rescramble the letters in people's names to discover their true nature."

Passengers on the *Mayflower* in 1620 included children with the names Remember, Wrestling, and Resolved. During colonial times, Puritans relied on the Bible or created their own message names for children, such as Fear-not, Much-Merceye, and Deliverance.

The U.S. Marshals Service Witness Security Program has given more than 18,000 witnesses and their families new identities, including new names. The program offers "a new life" to government witnesses whose testimony against major criminals endangers their lives.

Many people name their cars—everything from Betsy and Sherman to Pig-Pen and Black Beauty. Experts say it's because we see cars as "alive" and animate since they move us from place to place. We also personalize and take pride in our cars in ways we don't treat most appliances. It's probably safe to say few of us refer to our toasters as "Tom."

It's considered unlucky to change the name of a boat or a ship. Many sailors who choose to rename their boats perform elaborate ceremonies to ward away ill fortune and appease the gods of the sea.

# Explore More!

## BOOKS

*All Over the Map: An Extraordinary Atlas of the United States* by David Jouris. Ten Speed Press, 1994.

*Bad Baby Names* by Michael Sherrod and Matthew Rayback. Ancestry Publishing, 2008.

*The Complete Book of Pet Names: An ASPCA Book* compiled and edited by George Greenfield. Andrews McMeel, 1997.

*Freakonomics: A Rogue Economist Explores the Hidden Side of Everything* by Steven D. Levitt and Stephen J. Dubner. William Morrow, 2006.

*From Altoids to Zima: The Surprising Stories Behind 125 Famous Brand Names* by Evan Morris. Fireside, 2004.

*Hawaiian Names . . . English Names* by Eileen M. Root. Press Pacifica, 1987.

*The Language of Names: What We Call Ourselves and Why It Matters* by Justin Kaplan and Anne Bernays. Simon and Schuster, 1997.

*The Name's Familiar: Mr. Leotard, Barbie, and Chef Boyardee* by Laura Lee. Pelican Publishing Company, 1999.

*What's in a Name? Everything You Wanted to Know* by Leonard R. N. Ashley. Genealogical Publishing Co., Inc., 1989.

*What's in a Name? Reflections of an Irrepressible Name Collector* by Paul Dickson. Merriam-Webster, Inc., 1996.

*When My Name Was Keoko* by Linda Sue Park. Clarion 2002.

*Where Have You Gone, Vince Dimaggio?* by Edward Kiersh. Bantam Books, 1983.

## DVD

*The Grace Lee Project*, a Women Make Movies release, directed by Grace Lee, 2005.

## WEB SITES

American Name Society: www.wtsn.binghamton.edu/ANS

BabyNames.com: www.babynames.com

Catchword Brand Name Development: www.catchwordbranding.com

Celebrate Your Name Week: http://celebrateyournameweek.googlepages.com/

Dean Vaughn's Total Retention Systems: www.deanvaughn.com

The Fred Society: www.fredsociety.com

fun-with-words.com (anagrams): www.fun-with-words.com/anagrams.html

Good Characters, Inc. (Chinese Names): www.goodcharacters.com

Happy Name Day: www.happynameday.com

How States Got Their Nicknames: www.50states.com/bio/nickname1.htm

Internet Anagram Server: http://wordsmith.org/anagram

MakeWords.com (creating screen names): www.makewords.com/screen-names.aspx

Native American articles (Blackfoot Indians): www.native-languages.org/composition/blackfoot-indians.html

Social Security Administration—Popular Baby Names: www.ssa.gov/OACT/babynames

United States Marshals Service (witness security program): http://usmarshals.gov/witsec

# 🔍 There's a Name for It

**ANEMONYMS:** names given to violent winds and storms

**BRAND:** the unique name of a product, service, or company, such as Nike

**CATCHWORD:** a word or phrase repeated for effect

**COINAGE:** the creation of new words

**DOMAIN NAME:** a unique name that identifies an Internet site, such as facebook.com

**FAMILY NAME:** a name that identifies a family (see surname)

**FORENAME:** a person's first or given name in most European and European-influenced countries, such as the United States and Australia

**HURRICANE NAMES:** see anemonyms

**INITIALS:** the first letters of each word in a person's full name

**INOA:** Hawaiian word for name

**LINGUISTICS:** the scientific study of language

**MAIDEN NAME:** a woman's family name before she marries

**MATRONYMIC:** a name derived from a person's mother or maternal ancestor

**NAME-LETTER EFFECT:** the phenomenon that occurs when people's preferences for their own name and initials influence decisions such as where they live, e.g., Jack in Jacksonville.

**NEOLOGISM:** a newly created word or term, typically used to name new inventions

**NICKNAME:** an altered form of a proper name, such as Chris for Christopher, or a descriptive name used in place of the real name

***NOMEN EST OMEN:*** Latin proverb (a name is an omen) implying that names are destiny

**ONOMASTICS:** the study of names and naming practices

**ONOMATOPHOBIA:** the fear of hearing or saying particular names

**PATRONYMIC:** a name derived from a person's father or paternal ancestor, such as Ericson, son of Eric

**PET NAME:** an affectionate nickname

**PROPER NOUN:** a noun that names a specific person, place, or thing, such as Hailey, Boston, or the Golden Gate Bridge

**PSYCHOLINGUISTICS:** the study of how we understand, interpret, and respond to language

**SURNAME:** the name a person shares with his or her family

**TRADE NAME:** the official business name of a company, such as Kellogg or General Mills

# Sources

## INTERVIEWS:

Cleveland Kent Evans, associate psychology professor at Bellevue University in Bellevue, Nebraska, past president of the American Name Society and author of *The Great Big Book of Baby Names: A Complete Guide from A to Z*, Publications, Ltd., 2006; Jennifer Moss, founder and CEO of BabyNames.com; Don L. F. Nilsen, co-president of the American Name Society and professor of English linguistics at Arizona State University; Carol Lombard, master's degree candidate in sociolinguistics at the University of South Africa; Jacque Lynn Schultz, senior director, ASPCA National Outreach; Gary Padgett, author of the "Monthly Global Tropical Cyclone Summaries" from Andalusia, Alabama; Burt Alper, principal, Catchword Brand Name Development Company; Andy Chuang, president, Good Characters, Inc.; Students Crystal Chasse, Jennifer Lane, and Zack Lane; Sheri Stritof, About.com Marriage guide; Dr. Lewis P. Lipsitt, professor emeritus of psychology, medical science, and human development, Brown University; David M. Bird, Ph.D., professor of wildlife biology, McGill University, Canada; Terry Godlove, professor of philosophy and religion at Hofstra University; Scott Speed, American race car driver; and Dean Vaughn, president, Dean Vaughn Learning Systems, Inc. and author of *How to Remember Anything: The Proven Total Memory Retention System*, St. Martin's Press, 2007.

## NEWSPAPER AND MAGAZINE ARTICLES:

"Alicia Keys," *Newsweek*, Nov. 10, 2007; "And the Worst Bad Baby Name is . . ." by John Tierney, *New York Times*, April 7, 2008; "The Baby-Name Business," by Alexandra Alter, *The Wall Street Journal*, June 22, 2007; "The Best Weird-Name Story Contest," by John Tierney, *New York Times*, March 10, 2008; "A Boy Named Sue, and a Theory of Names," by J. Marion Tierney, *New York Times*, March 11, 2008; "Gee, That's an Odd Name, Ever Think of Acting?" by Jill Gerston, *New York Times*, May 18, 1997; "Hello, My Name Is Unique," by Carlin Fiora, *Psychology Today*, March/April 2004; "Jim Killeen: The Man Who Found Himself," by Monica Hesse, *Washington Post*, Aug. 13, 2007; "Judge Orders Kids to Legally Change Their Names," The Associated Press, July 24, 2008; "Living Life as Donald Duck," by Jane Elliott, *BBC News*, Jan. 3, 2005; "Not Your Father's Nicknames When Teens Talk to Parents," by Ellen Freeman Roth, *Boston Globe*, June 28, 2008; "Ms. Rose, by Any Other Name, Might Still Be a Florist," by Sam Roberts, *New York Times*, March 27, 2005; "The Name Game: In the Philippines, Quirky Monikers Stick," *Psychology Today*, Jan/Feb 2008; "Names That Match Forge a Bond on the Internet," by Stephanie Rosenbloom, *New York Times*, April 10, 2008; "Teens May Want to Leave Witty Screen Names Behind," by Nicole Sweeney, *Milwaukee Journal*

Sentinel, March 6, 2004; "What's in a Name," by Greg Langlois, *Perspectives: Research, Scholarship, and Creativity at Ohio University*, Autumn/Winter 1998; "What's the Name of That Lake? It's Hard to Say," by Pam Belluck, *The New York Times*, Nov. 20, 2004; "Why Stars Name Babies Moxie, Moses and Apple," by Alex Williams, *New York Times*, April 16, 2006; and "Will You Vote for Wonder Girl, Maverick, or Barry?" by Terry Stawar, *The Meadville Tribune*, March 31, 2008.

## ADDITIONAL RESOURCES:

"The Power of Names," The Word Nerds (podcast), April 23, 2005; "BabyCenter® Survey Finds Most New Parents Believe Their Child's Name Will Contribute to Success in Life," Press Release, BabyCenter, LLC, San Francisco, March 4, 2008; "Information on Icelandic Surnames," Ministry of Justice and Ecclesiastical Affairs at http://eng.domsmalaraduneyti.is/information/nr/125, Jan. 22, 2002; "What's in a Name?" by Deirdre McNamer, *Social Graces: Words of Wisdom on Civility in a Changing Society (Town & Country)*, Hearst, 2002; "The Icelandic Language," Ministry of Foreign Affairs at www.iceland.is/history-and-culture/Language; "Names and -Nyms," presentation by Don L. F. Nilsen and Alleen Pace Nilsen, co-presidents of the American Name Society; "Chinese surname shortage sparks rethink," *People's Daily Online*, June 20, 2007; "The Origin of Chinese Surnames," *Peoples' Daily Online*, Oct. 30, 2006; "Celebrity Baby Names" and "Celebrity Real Names" at BabyNames.com; "Hybrid Dogs," Dog Breed Info Center at www.dogbreedinfo.com; *Nicknames and Sobriquets of U.S. Cities, States, and Counties (Third Edition)* by Joseph Nathan Kane and Gerard L. Alexander. The Scarecrow Press, Inc., 1979; "Worldwide Tropical Cyclone Names," National Weather Service, National Hurricane Center, www.nhc.noaa.gov/about names.shtml; Famous Name Changes—Corporations, www.famousnamechanges.net; "Internet & American Life: Teens & Their Friends," by The Pew Internet & American Life Project, January 2007; Name Changes Frequently Asked Questions at www.nolo.com; "The Doctor's (and other health care practitioners) Names List," compiled by Mari Stoddard, University of Arizona: www.u.arizona.edu/~stoddard/doctor.htm; "Best of the best sports nicknames," ESPN.com Page 2, http://espn.go.com/page2/s/list/nicknames/bestofbest/010628.html; "Nicknames" and "Is Your Name Your Destiny," by Robert Needlman, M.D., F.A.A.P., Dr. Spock Company Web site at www.drspock.com; "Why do people name their cars? Driving Miss Daisy, or Jimmy, or Foo Foo," CarTest! Car Reviews Web site at www.cartest.ca/why_do_people_name_their_car.htm, Oct. 5, 2006. "Judge Bans 'Talula Does the Hula From Hawaii'" by The Associated Press, www.abcnews.go.com, July 24, 2008.

# ꟾ Index

## A

## B

## C

## D

## E

## F

Onomastics, 8

Onomatophobia, 55

# P

Patronymics, 17

Personal characteristics and names, 18

Pet names, 22–24

    tips on naming, 23–24

Philippines, nicknames in, 51

Place names, 25–26

    longest, 27

Professionals and names, 48

# R

Religions and names, 8

Remembering names, 53–54

# S

Screen personas, 39

Sense of identity and Blackfoot names, 16

Ship names, changing, and bad luck, 56

*Siksika* (Blackfoot), 15

Social disabilities and names, 12–13

Sport heroes nicknames, 52

State nicknames, 55

Surnames, 17–18

    Chinese, 20–21

*Surnom* (French for surname), 17

# T

Theronyms, 32

Topographical names, 18

Toponyms, 25–26

# U

U.S. Marshals Service Witness Security

    Program, 56

U.S. National Weather Service, 29–30

Unusual names, 12

# W

Washington, George, and his effect on

    names, 18

Witness Security Program, 56

Word pictures and remembering

    names, 53

World Meteorological Organization

    (WMO), 28, 30

# Y

Yahoo, 32

Yao Ming, 20

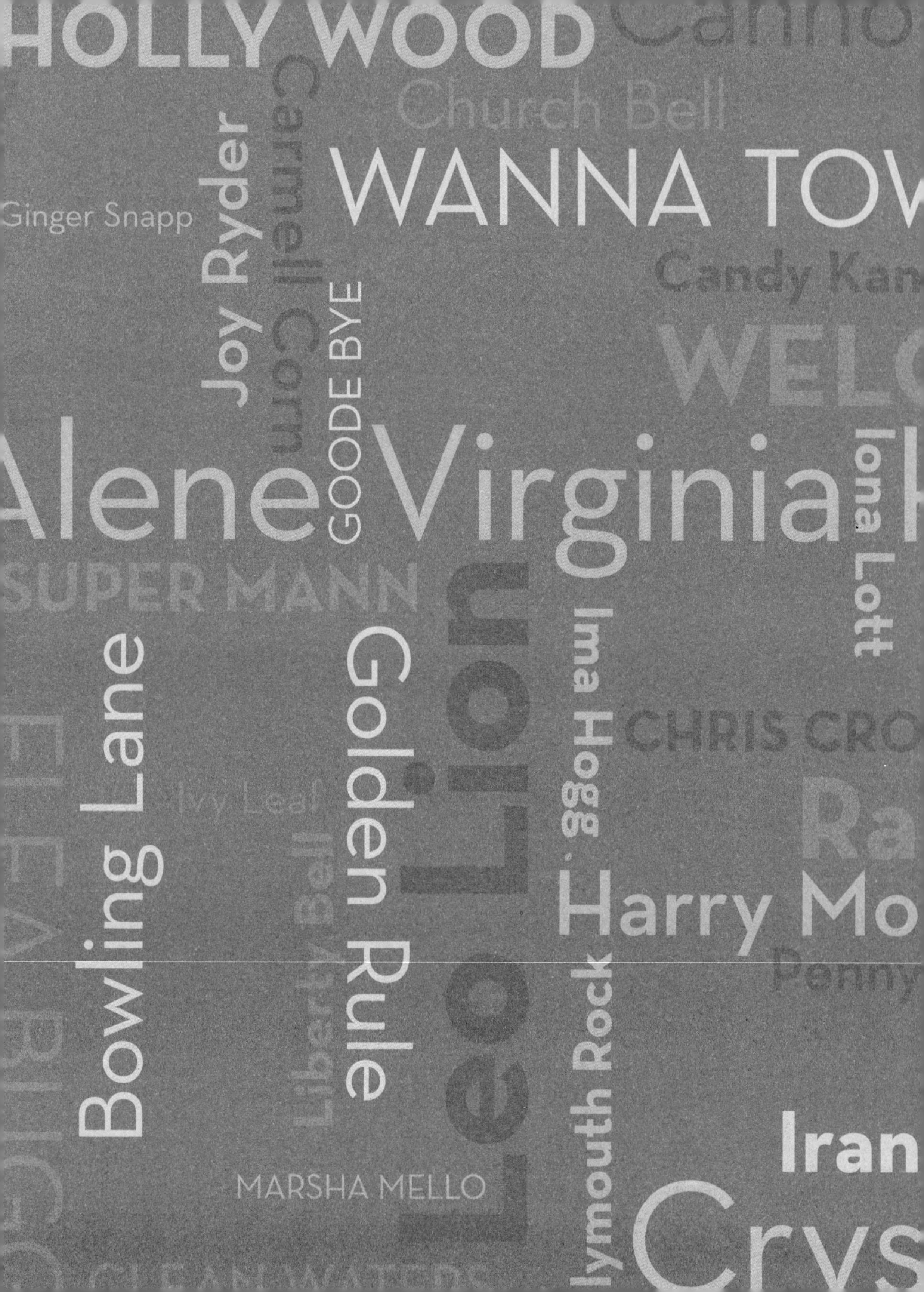

HOLLYWOOD

Canno

Church Bell

WANNA TOW

Ginger Snapp

Candy Kan

Joy Ryder

Carmell Corn

GOODE BYE

WELC

Virginia

Iona Lott

Alene

SUPER MANN

Golden Rule

Leo Lion

Ima Hogg

CHRIS CRO

Bowling Lane

Ra

ELEARBIGG

Ivy Leaf

Liberty Bell

Harry Mo

Penny

lymouth Rock

Iran

MARSHA MELLO

Crys

CLEAN WATERS